CONTENTS

THE ALMANACK OF STANLEY DRUCKENMILLER

Upgraded Brain © 2022

RUI ZHI DONG

NOTE

This has been built from Stanley Druckenmiller's interviews, tweets, speeches, books about him and transcripts over the years.

Interpretations change over time and quotes have been taken out of context.

Every attempt is made to present Druckenmiller in his own words. Having said that, not all sources have been primary so please interpret with a grain of salt.

This book has been organized in a way to give you easy access to Druckenmiller's unique perspective into markets, life, and business by dividing them into byte-sized chunks.

ABOUT STANLEY DRUCKENMILLER

Stanley Druckenmiller may be one of the greatest compounding money machines in history. He managed to achieve about a *40% average annual return* on a multi-billion dollar hedge fund over 25 years during his time at Quantum and a *30% average annual return* on his Duquesne Capital Management over 30 years. And *both* without a single down year.

Disappointed with his economics program at university, he decided to drop out and work as an analyst at the Pittsburgh National Bank. Within just a year, he's promoted to director of equity research and then promoted *again* within a year after that when the division head leaves the bank.

Two years later in 1980, at the age of 28, Stan starts Duquesne Capital Management.

In 1986, Dreyfus recruits Druckenmiller to be a fund manager while allowing him to continue running his own Duquesne fund.

By this time, Druckenmiller had developed his multi-asset approach with a mixture of bonds, commodities, currencies and stocks, trading on both the long and short side.

After burning out at Dreyfus and having a chance to fulfill his desire of working for his idol, George Soros, Druckenmiller left Dreyfus in 1988 and joined the Quantum Fund.

Together, they pioneered what's known today as macro trading, and the rest was history.

Soros eventually left the management of his fund to Druckenmiller while he went to pursue philanthropy in Eastern Europe.

Of the tremendous success at the Quantum Fund, Sebastian Mallaby, the author of *More Money Than God*, said Soros was more of a coach and that "Druckenmiller deserves 95 percent of the credit."

Druckenmiller left Quantum in 2000 and concentrated fulltime on Duquesne Capital until closing it in 2010, stating that, "While the joy of winning for clients is immense, for me the disappointment of each interim drawdown over the years has taken a cumulative toll that I cannot continue to sustain."

TIMELINE

1953: Born in Pittsburgh, Pennsylvania

1975: BA in English and economics from Bowdoin College

1977: Dropped out of a 3-year Ph.D. program in economics at the University of Michigan to accept a position as an analyst for Pittsburgh National Bank

1981: Founded Duquesne Capital Management

1986: Joins Dreyfus Fund

1988: Joins Quantum Fund

2000: Leaves Quantum Fund

2010: Closes Duquesne Capital Management

HARD WORK

I was pretty lazy in college and I never considered myself a particularly hard worker.

But I'm so passionate about our business that it's almost like a compulsive gambler that has a way to channel his compulsion.

The fact that every event in the world affects some security price somewhere and the fact that I'm so intellectually stimulated trying to imagine the world 12-18 months from now versus the way it looks in the present, and security prices, how it would affect that.

I just find it so stimulating that it makes everyone think I'm a hard worker because I'm attracted to the game. In this game, I am a hard worker but I actually think there is a life lesson there.

I've seen young people who when they find their life passion, who had kind of looked like they're lazy or lost become very driven. I just happen to be passionate about this particular discipline. I don't know if I have a hard work ethic but that's the end result of my passion.

BIAS

I have a bearish bias — I know it.

One of my jobs is to manage myself and know that bias exists.

I have a bearish bias for 45 years that I have had to work around.

I like darkness.

EMOTION

You're constantly fighting your own emotions.

My first boss had this saying, *The higher they go, the cheaper they look.*

There's something weird where when a security goes up, every bone in your body wants to buy more of it.

And when it goes down, you're fighting making yourself not sell it. It's just the nature of the beast.

You have to constantly remind yourself why you own that security.

Just because it's going down, doesn't necessarily mean you should sell it.

If it's going down, it definitely means you should reevaluate your thesis, but it doesn't mean you should sell it.

And you cannot get crazy when it's going up.

Probably the biggest mistake I ever made in the business was in January of 2000 after riding that tech boom to a tee and making billions of dollars in '99 I sold everything out in January, I had a couple of internal portfolio managers at Soros who didn't sell out and they made 30% after I sold.

I just couldn't stand it anymore and I'm watching them make all this money everyday and for two days I'm ready to pick up the phone and buy this stuff back.

I pick up the phone and I buy them -- I might have missed the top of the dot-com bubble by an hour.

I ended up losing $3 billion on that trade alone.

It was all because I got emotional and dropped every tool of discipline I ever had.

Somebody says well what did you learn from it? I just said I learned nothing -- I learned that 25 years ago.

You can talk about not being emotional but it takes incredible discipline to act on that.

CAREER ADVICE

I fell in love with investing really right out of graduate school. I'll never forget my first interview. The guy asked me where I want to be in ten years. I said intellectually stimulated. I didn't get the job — he thought I was an idiot.

The number one necessary condition woud be to do something you're passionate about.

Particularly in this business, the people that love it like me, are so addicted to it and so intellectually stimulated by it, if you're not and you're in it for the money, you have no chance competing with these people.

They're going to outwork you, they're going to outexecute you.

I think it's probably true in a lot of professions but let's not forget that if you're American, you're probably going to spend 60 or 70 hours a week minimum working. If you're in the job for the money and not because you love it, you just blew 70 hours a week on the happiness quotient, that's pretty rough.

So I would tell a 20 year old, follow your passion.

I was just lucky. I followed my passion.

My mother-in-law says I'm an idiot savant, that I wouldn't be good at anything else, but I would do this for $50,000 a year -- I really would. I just love it. And I hate to see young people get trapped in something.

If you're early on in your career and they give you a choice between a great mentor or higher pay, take the mentor every time. It's not even close. And don't even think about leaving that mentor until your learning curve peaks.

I had learned a tremendous amount just in my conversations with Soros. George Soros had become my idol. He seemed to be about twenty years ahead of me in implementing the trading philosophy I had adopted: holding a core group of stocks long and a core group of stocks short and then using leverage to trade S&P futures, bonds, and currencies.

I thought it was a no-lose situation. The worst thing that could happen was that I would join Soros and he would fire me in a year—in which case I would have received the last chapter of my education.

I would also say keep an open mind.

I started at Bowdoin as an English major, I took economics just so I could read the paper intelligently.

I went to get a Ph.D. in economics and I went there and I said, these people are crazy. They're trying to shove the economy into a math formula. It doesn't make any sense. Then I worked construction for 6 months. I got kind of a weak upper body so that didn't work out for me.

Then I went to the bank and I found out what I was just in love with it.

I came in at 6 in the morning and stayed until 8 at night. Remember this was a bank, not a brokerage firm at which such hours represent normal behavior.

So try stuff out and if you're not really really engaged during the day and you're not happy, move on to something else.

There's something out there for everybody.

I would not let money be the driver of the equation. That can lead to a lot of not maximizing what I call the happiness quotient. It's the most important quotient of your life.

My real passion is in macro.

My dream would be to find a successor to run the entire equity part of my family office and have me fiddling around in the macro and acting like the old talking head sage and coach to him.

I think I would die if I couldn't have some connection with the investment market and the markets during the day.

First of all, I'm not very good at golf, I like doing stuff that I'm good at. No one likes being a loser.

I think I'll probably go to the grave doing this stuff.

EARLY DAYS AT THE BANK

I really had no idea what kind of job I would end up with. Most of the people who entered the management training program at the bank had an immediate goal of becoming a loan officer.

I thought that I had been doing pretty well when the head of the loan department informed me that I would make a terrible loan officer.

The director of investments was Speros Drelles, the person who had hired me. He was brilliant, with a great aptitude for teaching, but he was also quite eccentric. When I was 25 and had been in the department for only about a year, he summoned me into his office and announced that he was going to make me the director of equity research.

This was quite a bizarre move, since my boss was about 50 years old and had been with the bank for over 25 years. Moreover, all the other analysts had

MBAs and had been in the department long than I had.

WHAT TO LEARN

I actually think the next 4-5 years are going to be tailored to the skillset that worked for me in the '80s and '90s which was all sorts of macro chaos and I would encourage them to learn all the asset categories and how they integrate.

In bear markets, that's when macro make all their money because that's when you used to have the biggest bond moves and the biggest currency moves. This stuff really moves in chaos. So a macro investor roots for chaos and we're all competitive fanatics.

If I was a tech investor, we had the internet wave, we had the cloud wave, cloud doesn't look like it's over yet, but I would certainly be looking into blockchain very deeply and the possible disruption it might take.

Back then, you had this incredible wave from '95 to 2000 while the internet was being built. What you have now is this incredible wave of digital transformation, particularly moving on to the cloud.

If you're a customer and you haven't moved to the cloud, you're dead. Because who you're competing against, they can just beat you because the technology is so important.

STREAKS

I believe in streaks. You see it in baseball, you see it in everything else, I see it in investing. Sometimes you're seeing the ball, sometimes you're not.

You can be far more aggressive when you're making good profits.

One of my number one jobs is to know when I'm hot or cold. When I'm hot, I'm suppose to turn the dial way up. Not say okay I'm up 40% this year, this will look good end of year, let's go take a break.

No you've got to make hay when you're hot.

And then when you're cold, the last thing you should do is make big bets to get back to even. You should tone yourself down.

So not only do I have to see the investment that really excites me, I also have to see myself sort of being in a good trading rhythm.

DOT-COM
BUBBLE

Monetary Policy was part of the issue in '99 when Greenspan decided he wanted to run an experiment where he let unemployment go below levels where it had historically been.

When you think about the fact that Netscape didn't really exist until '95 so other than some nerdy professors back in the early 80s, no one even had email. Literally the internet was just sort of being built.

The big winners in '99 were companies like Sun Micro and Cisco that were building the guts of the internet.

So what happened was the growth was so rapid and valuations combined with some easy money got baked into those growth rates as far as the eye could see.

Think of the internet infrastructure like the railroads 150 years ago and think of the tech stocks as a company selling railroad ties building the guts of the internet.

While you're building the railroad, your sales are going up 50, 60, 70 percent a year. But once the railroad is built, your growth not only doesn't go up 70%, it goes down because on a rate of change basis, you don't need any more railroad ties.

What none of us saw, me included, in early 2000 where a lot of these companies with estimates of 50, 60, 70 percent for the next 2 or 3 years, their business was literally about to collapse.

The NASDAQ went down 95%, not 30 because you had this combination of inflated values, way overestimated earnings out there and then earnings collapsed.

Back then a lot of value managers were virtually going out of business right at the end of 2000.

One of the greatest investors of all time, Julian Robertson, who was long value and short these crazy tech names, he basically threw in the towel and said he couldn't take it anymore and stopped managing money in the early 2000s.

But what happened in the next 3-5 years was incredible.

Companies like Phelps Dodge Copper went up 6-8 times for the old industrial stuff. So everything that Julian was long went up many fold and the tech stocks went down a lot.

BEST FAANG

I've always answered that with Amazon and Microsoft.

I've never really believed that Apple had the innovation to take you to the next level and was mainly a hardware company.

They obviously have morphed into this services app company.

That's the one I haven't talked about being a monopoly but when you look at monopoly behavior, charging a 30% rent to all these little companies seem a little extreme whereas Amazon and Microsoft — they basically don't raise prices.

My number one would be Amazon and number two would be Microsoft.

Google could have a big pop ironically if the government breaks them up because they core search business is literally the best business I've ever seen.

But they keep trying all of this experimental stuff that challenges shareholder value. But those guys are so rich that they're more interested in changing the world right now, so good for them.

TAIWAN

I'm worried about Taiwan.

I can't imagine Xi Jinping not going to try something.

That's big stuff. That's not some little thing where Yemen is fighting Saudi Arabia.

If you were to get worried about the United States and China, that could be an exogenous event. It could get quite nasty.

CHINA RELATIONS

Who knew that probably the best US-China relations we'd see for the next 25 years would be under Trump.

What was a cold war seems to be turning into a hot war.

DIVERSIFICATION

When I look at all the investors of very large reputations — Warren Buffet, Carl Icahn, George Soros — they all only have one thing in common.

And it's the exact opposite of what they teach in a business school.

They make large concentrated bets where they have a lot of conviction. They're not buying 35 or 40 names and diversifying.

Icahn a few years ago put $5 billion into Apple and I don't think he was worth more than $10 billion when he did that.

When I went into tell Soros that I was going to short 100% of the fund in the British Pound against the Deutsche Mark, he looked at me with great disdain because he thought the story was good enough that I should be doing 200% cause it was a once in a generation opportunity.

So A, they concentrate their holdings, B, concentration really gets your attention and in my thinking decreases your overall risk. Because where you tend to be in trouble is when you have 35 or 40 names and you stop paying attention to one. If you have big massive positions, it has your attention.

My favorite quote of all time is Mark Twain:

Put all your eggs in one basket and watch the basket carefully.

I tend to think that's what great investors do.

In business school, they teach that if you're highly diversified, you have less risk than if you're highly concentrated. I don't believe that at all.

As an investor, when I think most people get into the most trouble is when they have stale longs or stale shorts.

When you've got 15-20% of your asset base, sometimes in macro positions I'll have 200 or 300%, believe me they're not getting stale. You have to have ruthless discipline, you're coming in everyday just, quoting Andy Grove, you could not be any more paranoid. You're constantly re-evaluating and I think it leads to an open mind.

I'm very much of the philosophy, which also creates its own discipline, is put all of your eggs in one basket and watch the basket very carefully.

I found time and time again that every investor has three or four big winners a year. Usually you know what they are. When you get in trouble is something when you're not entirely focused.

When you put 50, 60, 70% of your assets or more in one asset class, trust me you're focused and you're more risk adverse than something where you might have 5 or 6% and have a blow up.

THE MOST IMPORTANT THING ABOUT STOCKS

I keep going back to my boss in Pittsburgh but I was an analyst and I analyzed retail.

I come in with my earnings estimate on Kmart and my earnings estimate on this company and that and he says, *Yeah but what's going to make the stock go up?*

And I said, *What do you mean?*

He says, *Everybody knows what you just told me. Keep looking. Keep looking.*

Finally I came back, and this has changed since then, if you graphed the change in food and energy prices, overtop the retail index, it was like clockwork.

Food and energy prices go up, retail relative stocks go down. It's not rocket science here. If you take discretionary spending and you increase the cost of it, she's got less money to buy a dress. And I watched that, it worked for 10 or 12 years, and then for some reason it stopped working.

There's an analysis of fundamentals which I completely endorse where you look at the balance sheet and try and figure out a couple of years from now what people are going to think about this company or the earnings are going to be different than they think now -- that kind of stuff.

Then there's all of the weird stuff like I just mentioned. If the stuff works, I'm going to go with it. I'm very open-minded -- I don't need to totally understand something if I've seen it work over and over again. But most of these things I understand.

What my mentor made me focus on what moves the stock price.

You can't just say, Stan, this is a great company and the earnings are great.

Tell me how people are going to think differently in 18 or 24 months about this situation than they're thinking now.

Do not invest in the present.

The present is not what moves stock prices.

Change moves them. I want you to try and envision a different world in a year and a half from now and where these security prices would trade versus now given the world you envision.

MULTIASSET STRATEGY

I think a lot of my performance has been because I'm flexible in terms of instruments I use, in terms of assets.

I'm not afraid of just playing bonds or currencies or this or that.

I think history would say in macro I'm probably an A + and in equities I'm probably a B —.

Equities are much more labor intensive.

There's only one yen, there's only one euro.

The fact that I can travel around five or six asset classes does a couple of things.

One, it can point you in the right direction and, if you really believe something, you can make big, big gains there.

Two, as a macroinvestor, currencies and bonds trade 24 hours a day and they're very liquid. You can change your mind which I've had to do a lot in my career because I've been wrong a lot in my career.

Three, and this is more subtle, it also gives you discipline not to be playing around in an area that's dangerous. If you're an equities only investor, it's your job to be in equities. If you have the latitude to say, "I'm just not going to play, it's too complicated" and you don't play in them.

Credit is a perfect example. I've never lost money big in credit because the only time I've ever had credit is when everything else is a complete debacle and we go ahead and buy a bunch of credit. Whereas if I was a credit investor, I would have had three or four down 30% years.

GROWTH STOCKS

The biggest money I've made in equities have been in growth stocks over time.

One of the cardinal rules I learned early on in venture capital is look where the kids are going.

I think I bought [Palantir] stock in '08 or '09. [Palantir] was a magnet for talent.

MARKET SIGNALS

The best economist I know is the inside of the stock market. I've always believed that markets are smarter than I am. They send out a message and if I listen to them properly, no matter how powerful my thesis, if they're screaming something else, it's telling me you've got to re-evaluate, you've got to re-evaluate, and you go back to it. You've got to be open-minded.

I found that the inside of the stock market had a very prescient message about future economic activity. For whatever reason, stocks tend to lead the fundamentals by somewhere between 6 and 12 months. You can even go beyond that and look at industries that lead the economy and industries that lagged the economy.

The obvious one that everyone knows about is housing -- it's traditionally being looked at as the leading industry.

Retail has a slightly capital goods lag and what

we've done historically is we do the macro by a compilation of listening to companies and doing a bottoms up analysis of industries that lead the economy and industries that lag the economy. And if the leading industries are turning up or turning down, that's a signal. That's worked beautifully historically.

The other signal which I have found quite prescient for markets is the bond market.

Unfortunately, the last 10 or 11 years the bond market has not signaled anything because the central banks took it upon themselves to manipulate bond prices.

10 year treasury has been the most important price in the world and they took that price out of the equation as a signal.

I don't think you get that tainting if you look inside the stock market.

You could get it in the stock market as a whole but if you do this approach where you look at industries — which lead, which lag -- and you put the puzzle together, it's been prescient over time and it's certainly allowed us to consistently the last 30 or 40 year outperform the Fed in economic forecasts.

You can just do the homebuilders themselves. With supposedly good fundamentals, they've all declined 50% from the high. Another industry that's been incredibly prescient has been trucking and they're down 40% from the high despite the fact that they're all reporting record earnings.

An industry that's not that much of a leader but it's more of a leader than a laggard is the retail industry. There's been a lot in the news lately whether it's been Walmart or other retail. That one is a little tainted because in Covid retail went to 100% of the wallet from about 85% because we weren't going outside and traveling and going to football games but even taking that into account, retail appears to be much weaker than it should be given what the so called GDP numbers are printing.

So right now there's a signal albeit early that there may be trouble ahead.

It's housing, retail, trucking.

You can't get too carried away and say that there will be a recession tomorrow morning.

A lot of these things have longer lead times like 6 months to a year.

Price versus news is a very weakened tool versus 20 years ago, much to my chagrin. I found it a great warning signal. That's been one thing I've had to adapt to.

You could almost always guarantee that if the economy looked great but the bonds were rallying, that meant the economy was not going to look so great. We use to call it price action versus news. It use to be an incredible indicator of security prices.

I've always made even higher returns in bear markets than bull markets. But the way I did it was pretty much ignore equities, buy bonds, buy treasuries and go home. Well, I've never been presented a cocktail where you have 8% inflation, you think the economy might weaken, and bond yields are 3%.

It's an analog with no precedent in history.

Bonds which have been my go to asset in terms of a recessionary bear market atmosphere, they may work but there's a good reason to believe that things may be different this time.

You can't get into black and white. You have to constantly innovate and not be a slave to past models.

We're now getting definitive signals that the economy may be weakening, particularly in the front end. And while I'm not comfortable owning bonds, I'm much less comfortable being short fixed income to the degree I was when it looked like a much better risk-reward.

Even stocks — so many companies have been de-rated by 60 or 70% and I've lived through enough bear markets that if you get aggressive in a bear market on the short side, you can get your head ripped off in rallies.

I'm coming in everyday and I'm looking at my screen but I'm pretty much taking a break waiting for a fat pitch. My anticipation is I will be going back to the short equity position at some point if the market affords me, if not hopefully I'll just sidestep a decline, that's not the worst thing in the world.

The fixed income market has become much more complicated. I'm lucky enough since I play in a lot of asset classes to have the luxury of not playing in one. I don't think I'll be playing much in that one going forward.

The currency market is incredibly interesting to me. I haven't been doing much there and I'm not currently positioned aggressively there. I will be surprised if at sometime in the next 6 months, I'm not short the dollar. $14 trillion has come in here because we were the first to tighten, there's a story about American exceptionalism. I'm not sure we're so exceptional anymore and if we are, I'm not sure I'm excited about what we're exceptional in. Foreign exchange looks interesting.

ALGOS AND SIGNALS

The algos coming in with very sophisticated models based on historical events and maybe stuff they're picking up on the internet about who's shopping or this kind of stuff and also on standard deviation away from price have come up with their own methodology of how to predict price movements and how to behave.

I do think that in today's world, you better know what they're doing. Particularly if you're in the trading business like I am. They influence markets and you have to know if a particular price move is happening because of them or if it's happening from more natural causes.

I grew up with, someone fundamentally likes a security and they buy it from somebody who fundamentally doesn't like the security and somehow the invisible hand spit out a very good answer and it was predictive over time.

I also learned over time that things would change and when the trends started to go up, that's when I'm supposed to plow in.

Well, the machines trading tend to have different motivations. They're not nearly as momentum oriented. Just when the trend may look like it's going up, it may be just some algo that's got some standard deviation or something going on and it has severely inhibited my ability to read the signals.

My first mentor, Speros Drelles, back in Pittsburgh used to say, 100 million Frenchmen can't be wrong.

That was his way of saying that the voice of the market was always correct and I need to listen to it. And it was true.

If a company was reporting great earnings and everybody loved it and the stock just didn't act well for 3 or 4 months, almost inevitably something happened that you didn't foresee 6 months down the road.

I'll never forget that Facebook had reported great

earnings, stock was like $122, opens $131 after hours, and three days later it's trading at $116. So the analysts come in and they're saying nothing's wrong, it's great.

I said, no kid, you're wrong. Something's going to come out. You just don't know it yet. Something terrible in the next three or four months. A year later, the stock is like $220. So that didn't mean anything.

Conversely, I can remember so many examples when a company would report bad earnings, it goes down 5% on huge volume and then closes up on the day. Almost invariably 3-6 months later, that stock was higher.

It doesn't mean anything anymore other than some hedge fund's being a wise guy or somebody's doing something.

The price signals that I learned, how to read and how to listen to, they certainly don't work the way they use to.

I still like price actions versus news but it use to be a

very, very important part of my process.

Now it's a much diminished part of my process and frankly it's made my job much more difficult and I'm thrilled I got rid of my clients. I'm going to have to learn how to do more fundamentals that I have historically.

I think the message over 8 or 9 months is still great. I just think over a week or two, you're getting noise that use to mean something and now it doesn't mean anything.

But they're still pretty good predicting ahead.

RISK MODELS

I've never used VaR [*ed. Value at Risk*].

We had to use it at Soros to get banking lines from great companies like Goldman Sachs.

But basically, very unsophisticated. I watch my PnL [*ed. profit and loss*] everyday. It would start acting in a strange manner relative to what I would expect out of the matrix and my antenna would go up.

I've always used my PNL because I found all those risk models — they're great until complete chaos happens and then all the correlations breakdown. They can suck you into a false sense of security.

If you're watching your PNL and your antennae are up, and you've been doing it for 30 or 40 years, I've found it a much better warning system than some of these mathematical models up there.

They're useful. They're just not useful when you really, really need something like that.

THE FEDERAL RESERVE

The Fed's mandate is maximize full employment over the longer term and price stability over the longer term.

To me, the way you achieve those objectives is not with boom bust cycles. And we continue to have these boom bust cycles.

One of the reasons is the Fed has confused what we're solving for, which is price stability and maximum employment, with using employment as an indicator. Employment is a lagging indicator so just because you want to maximize employment doesn't mean when the unemployment rate is low, you can't back off. Most recessions were preceded by a very low unemployment rate. That's what you do. You run out of capacity.

The Fed, when they look at the stock market and financial indicators, probably they're just looking at the S&P.

The S&P is a mirage because if you look inside the stock market, the cyclical elements of the economy, particularly the front end cyclicals, show a completely different picture than the defensive parts of the stock market.

Auto stocks are down 30%, building stocks are down 35%, banks are down 25%, the Russell 2000 is down over 20%, retail equities are down over 20%. So how in the world can the S&P only be down 10 or 11%?

It's because utilities, staples and pharmaceuticals, which are economically defensive, are actually up.

This is the same situation I've used cycle after cycle.

What I would like the Fed to do is get out of the forward guidance business completely. I don't know what it does other than tie their hands.

To be frank, given their record, it's kind of embarrassing when you forward guide and then you're stuck with a guidance that's not necessarily appropriate.

I grew up in a world where the Fed didn't spoon feed you everyday. You just come in and it turns out that they've raised rates or they're tweaking the repo rate or something, and we seemed to do fine without the spoon feeding.

Unprecedented Stimulus

The story of the time [in 2021] was inflation was 1.7, and we were buying 120 billion bonds a month.

This was post-vaccine, successful vaccine, because inflation was 1.7 instead of 2. We're taking this massive gamble where you threaten 40 years of credibility with inflation, and you're blowing up the wildest raging asset bubble I've ever seen.

I knew that the worst economies happen post asset bubbles. The '30s here, post '89 in Japan after the housing bubble blew up here. So that's what I went on.

The Fed did 2 trillion in QE after vaccine confirmation. You had the strongest momentum in employment in history on a rate of change basis.

At the same time their partner in crime, the administration, was doing more fiscal stimulus, again post-vaccine, after it was clear emergency measures weren't needed, than we did in the entire great financial crisis.

I'm not talking about before the vaccine, I'm talking about after. It turned out I was right. I've been wrong plenty of times in my life. The Fed was wrong. They made a big mistake. It's not so much that they were wrong. I've been wrong a lot. It's the risk-reward bet they made.

Asymmetric Bet

If you look at what the Fed did, the radical gamble they took to get inflation up 30 basis points from 1.7 to 2, it's to me sort of a risk-reward bet.

You bet 1 to lose 40? And they lost.

And who really lost?

Poor people in the United States ravaged by inflation, the middle class, and my guess is the U.S.

economy for years to come because of the extent of the asset bubble in time and duration and breadth it went on.

It's Transitory

What was particularly mind boggling to me, two to three months later, inflation takes off, it's no longer a theory.

It's actually happening.

We come up with this ridiculous theory of transitory. We have 5 trillion in fiscal stimulus, we have 5 trillion in QE. Janet Yellen is running down the TGA account, so that's another trillion in stimulus.

The monetary framework in the fall of 2020, they were no longer going to forecast.

They were going to be data-dependent and wait until they see the whites of inflation's eyes.

So guess what? They saw the whites of their eyes. And what did they do? They forecast that it was going to be transitory.

When you make a mistake, you've got to admit you're wrong and move on. That nine or ten months that they just sat there and bought 120 billion in bonds, I think the repercussions of that are going to be with us for a long, long time.

Slaying The Dragon

But right now, I like everything I'm hearing out of the Fed, and I hope they finish the job.

They made a big mistake. They seem to have owned it, but it's easy to own it when employment is strong.

Let's see what happens if we get a hard landing. I just hope they stick to their guns because this stuff was terrible in the 1970s. You have to slay the dragon. And the chair is right.

You're probably going to have some pain.

[If] the Fed engineers something here that we have some short-term pain for, to me they're doing the right thing and it will be worth it.

The risk is because it was preceded by 30 trillion dollars of QE, that it turns into something worse.

I'm not predicting that, but I'm open-minded to it.

WHEN TO SELL

You've got to have to know how and when to take a loss.

Soros is the best loss taker I've ever seen. He doesn't care whether he wins or loses on a trade. If a trade doesn't work, he's confident enough about his ability to win on other trades that he can easily walk away from the position.

I've been in business since 1976 as a money manager, I've never used a stop loss. Not once. Dumbest concept I've ever heard. It goes down 15%, I'm automatically out.

But I've also never hung onto a security if the reason I bought it has changed, and that's when you need to sell.

If I buy X security for A, B, C and D reasons, and those are no longer valid, whether I have a loss or a gain, that stock doesn't know whether you have a loss or gain.

It is not important. Your ego is not what this is about. What this is about is your making money.

So if I have a thesis and it doesn't bear out, which happens often with me, I'm often wrong, just get out and move on because if you're using a multi-disciplined approach, you can find something else.

There's no reason to hang on to any security where you don't have great conviction in it.

CYCLICALS

I think fundamentals are fundamentals.

When companies are losing money, capacity is always going to shrink and margins are going to look better in 3 years.

When companies are overearning, margins are going to come down in 3 years. I think all of that stuff will be out there.

One of my first group was chemicals.

They were really easy. When they were losing money, you were suppose to buy them because everybody shut capacity down the next 2 or 3 years but people are still going to need chemicals.

And when they made a bunch of money, they use to announce all of these capacity expansions so you knew what was going to happen.

The ideal time to sell these stocks is when there are lots of announcements for new plants, not when the earnings turn down.

The reason for this behavioral pattern is that expansion plans mean that earnings will go down in two to three years, and the stock market tends to anticipate such developments.

Well I've taken those lessons forward 30 or 40 years and they still work.

SHORTS

The shorts have tended to be in my book centered around the cyclical and value area.

In tech, we've been long the disrupters and short the disrupted which has worked beautifully over 2 years.

We've been short all of the financials because why in the world would you buy a group that needs rates to go up to own it.

The last time I checked, banks and equities don't do well with rates going up.

ENERGY

Very nervous because it's not the unique thesis it was 6 months ago.

We still own energy and other commodities. Ukraine gave that trade an extended life. Because of the transition to ESG, we look to be short energy for 5-10 years so that could last a while.

The reason we're still there is we just see this thing as more sustainable because of ESG and all the reasons we all know about that it can last a while and that doesn't seem to have been priced in the stocks.

But it's not a classic Duquesne play because it's now become widely recognized.

But I don't just sell something because people talk about pain trade — I don't care about pain trade this or that. We think these companies are still cheap relative to what we see a year or two out.

The big problem would obviously be if you have a horrendous worldwide recession but we'll look for demand destruction in energy but so far we don't see it.

TECH

These cloud companies to me looked mobile 10 years ago.

They're in the second inning of a nine-inning game as corporate America has to convert to the cloud.

I'm talking about Microsoft, ServiceNow, SalesForce, that kind of stuff.

They're very high-priced but to me if we're going to a 1-2% growth rate and interest rates are benign, and they're worth more in that environment than they are in a 3.5% environment because they're going to grow the same rate either way.

You could argue that if we get in a mild recession, demand for their product goes up because it's a way to cut costs.

BUY FIRST, ANALYZE LATER

You just don't have the time you had when I got in the business when you hear a good idea.

If you wait 2 or 3 weeks, a lot of times now believe it or not, 60 or 70% of the move will have taken place.

Maybe not the long term move but entry price is important and it's important psychologically as you add over time.

I've just found particularly the last 10 or 20 years, you just don't have time anymore to do deep-dive analysis.

You do but if you have the intuition, you buy it and then you do the analysis, and then get rid of it if it doesn't pan out as oppose to wait and do the analysis.

When you enter it, there's no story out there, so

hopefully in 10 days if you're wrong, there's still no story.

There's not going to be some bear story because the guy's giving you a bull story. But if there is a bull story, it's quite likely that someone's going to discover it over the next 2 or 3 weeks.

These analysts go to dinner with each other like 4 nights a week and tout their ideas and, a lot of times, they don't wait for their portfolio manager because they're trying to make themselves look good with the other guys at dinner too. I use to do that when I had a lot more energy.

If some analyst come in with a great idea, I don't just buy it and tell them to go do the analysis. But if they have an idea that appeals to me intuitively and I really like it and it might fit in with the macro matrix then it might tick a bunch of boxes.

VOLATILITY

Volatility is only good if it's part of a trend and it's giving you entry points within a trend.

We're getting volatility with no trend. When you're going up and down but there's no real trend, that's a nightmare.

You might think that a volatility move is the beginning of a trend and get yourself whipsawed.

COVID SHORTS

I don't have the nerves that I use to have but this was the best short selling period I've ever seen in the last year or two because never before were there such obvious overearners.

Like particularly brick and mortar retail. You see companies that don't grow for 15 years and all of a sudden, the stocks have quadrupled. It didn't take a rocket scientist to figure out 2 or 3 years from now, people will start traveling again, companies will overspend, all this stuff that typically happens.

Covid was a unique opportunity.

I think the fact that all this new money came into the market made it even more unique and exaggerated in terms of opportunity.

Big tech was widely regarded as overearners in covid, and maybe they were early on, but it was so widely broadcast.

The true overearners were things to me like retail, trucking, or today, ocean shipping companies that just have these massive margin.

I can envision a world where world trade is not booming in 2 years by the way.

It was obvious who the overearners were in that first 6 months. All you had to do was go down the chain and pick them off the last year and a half.

It's gotten much harder because 80% of that set has is already down to a place where I'd rather not play.

SUBPRIME LENDING

I had a brilliant analyst from Lehman Brothers come in and lay out the whole subprime thing for me and said by the 3rd quarter of '07 all hell is going to break loose.

By the time he left that meeting, over the next 2 days I shorted everything to do with housing and I was wrong for 6 months and it drove me crazy.

But the analysis was consistent.

The deeper we dug, the more confident we got.

I still believe had Bernanke recognized what was going on when 20-50 money managers did in early to mid 2007, that this was not a little $100 billion dollar problem that was containable but that it was a disaster looming, and had he cut 6-9 months earlier, we would have had a recession but I don't know whether we would have had a financial crisis.

And we certainly wouldn't have had the financial

consequences we've had.

I met with the Treasury Secretary in 2005 and laid out the whole thing.

CRYPTOS

I've evolved on this. I've said more than once, crypto and Bitcoin are a solution in search of a problem.

What the hell are these people all looking for? We already have that — it's called the dollar.

For the first movement in Bitcoin, I think it went from 50 bucks to $17,000, I just sat there aghast. I wanted to buy it everyday it was going up even though I didn't think much of it. I just couldn't stand the fact that it was going up and I didn't own it.

I never owned it from $50 to $17,000 and I felt like a moron. Then it goes back down to $3,000 again and a couple of things happened.

This is consistent with the fundamental and then let's make something go up or down. Solution in search of a problem. I found the problem. We did the CARES Act and Chairman Powell started crossing all sorts of red lines in terms of what the Fed would do and wouldn't do.

The problem was Jay Powell and world central bankers going nuts and making fiat money even more questionable than it had already been when I used to own gold. Then the second thing that happened is I got a call from Paul Jones and he says to me, do you know that when Bitcoin went from $17,000 to $3,000, 86% of the people that owned it at $17,000 never sold it?

Well this was huge in my mind. Here's something with a finite supply, 86% of the owners are religious zealots. I mean, who holds something that goes from $17,000 to $3,000 and it turns out that 86% of the people never sold it?

And I had this new central bank craziness phenomena.

So it goes up to 6,000 in the middle of the last spring and I got to buy some of those just because these kids on the west coast are already worth more than I am and they're going to be making a lot more money than me in the future. For some reason they're looking at this thing the way I've always looked at gold which is a store of value if I don't trust fiat currencies.

And then the fact that it had been around 13 years and it had become a brand. I tried to buy $100 million at 6,200 and it took me 2 weeks to buy $20 million. I bought it all around 6,500 I think and I said, this is ridiculous. It takes me 2 weeks -- I can buy that much gold in 2 seconds. So like an idiot I stopped buying it, next thing I knew, the thing's trading at 36,000.

I took my cost and then some out of it, and I still own some of it, my heart's never been in it, I'm a dinosaur.

Once it started moving and these institutions start adopting it, I can see the old elephant trying to get through the keyhole and they can't fit through in time.

I own this company called Palantir and I see their announced with their earnings today that they're going to start accepting Bitcoin and they may invest — that's happening all over the place. And you know, this thing is never going to have more than 21 million -- it's a fixed supply. I think because it's a brand that's been around for 14 years, because of the finite supply, it has sort of won this store of value game.

Is it going to beat the other cryptos in terms of digital gold store of value? I would say that it's going to be very very tough to unseat.

Then I go to what I call the commerce facilitators which obviously the lead in smart contracts and that kind of stuff would be ethereum. There I'm a little more skeptical of whether they can hold their position.

It reminds me a little of Yahoo! before Google came along. Google wasn't that much faster than Yahoo! but it didn't need to be, All it needed to be was a little bit faster and the rest is history.

One of the ways we've always invested in the private sector is to try and figure out where the engineering kids from Stanford and Brown and MIT are going. So many of them are in love with crypto and that's where they're going.

I'm worried about the talent that's like 23-28 years

old. Somebody we don't even know who they are yet, come up with a payment system or whatever and unseat things. I don't know. My guess is the winner in the commerce facilitator whether you want to call it payments or smart contract or whatever, there's a good chance that that currency hasn't even been invented yet.

There's a strong correlation between crypto and the NASDAQ. I don't think it takes a genius to figure out why. So I'm looking at it as an indicator that way.

Everything that Charlie Munger says about it, I'm sympathetic to. Everything that Bill Miller says about it, I'm sympathetic to.

That's a movie that has yet to be played out and one that I don't want to bet on with conviction. I will be very surprised if blockchain isn't a real force in our economy say 5 years from now to 10 years from now and not a major disrupter with companies that will have been founded between now and then and that will do very well and also challenge things like our financial companies and do a lot of disruption.

So I find crypto interesting.

I could see crypto currency having a big role in a Renaissance because people just aren't going to trust the central banks.

GOLD VS BITCOIN

If you believe we're going to have irresponsible monetary policy and inflation going forward, if it's in a bull phase, you want to own bitcoin, but if it's in a bear phase, you want to own gold.

If we're going to have an inflationary bull market, I want to own bitcoin more than gold and if I thought we're going to have a bear market stagflation type tying, then I want to own more gold.

SIZING

People ask me what I learned from George Soros.

I thought when I went there, I was going to learn what made the Yen and Deutsche Mark go up and down, and that kind of thing.

No what I learned was sizing is probably 70-80% of the equation.

It's not whether you're right or wrong, it's how much you make when you're right and how much you lose when you're wrong.

The few times that Soros has ever criticized me was when I was really right on a market and didn't maximize the opportunity.

As an example, shortly after I had started working for Soros, I was very bearish on the dollar and put on a large short position against the Deutsche mark. The position had started going in my favor, and I felt rather proud of myself. Soros came into my office, and we talked about the trade.

"How big a position do you have?" he asked.

"One billion dollars," I answered.

"You call that a position?" he said dismissingly.

He encouraged me to double my position. I did, and the trade went dramatically further in our favor.

Soros has taught me that when you have tremendous conviction on a trade, you have to go for the jugular.

It takes courage to be a pig. It takes courage to ride a profit with huge leverage.

As far as Soros is concerned, when you're right on something, you can't own enough.

HEDGING

I don't really like hedging.

To me, if something needs to be hedged, you shouldn't have a position in it.

RELATIONSHIP WITH GEORGE SOROS

The first 6 months of the relationship were fairly rocky.

While we had similar trading philosophies, our strategies never meshed.

In my opinion, George Soros is the greatest investor that ever lived. But even being coached by the world's greatest investor is a hindrance rather than a help if he's engaging you actively enough to break your trading rhythm. You can't have two cooks in the kitchen; it doesn't work.

BREAKING THE BANK OF ENGLAND

The beauty of the pound trade was that it was a one way bet -- it was either going to be flat or we're going to make 15 or 20%.

If I can't figure out whether I'm going to make 10% or lose 10%, I look elsewhere.

It is my favorite currency.

30 years ago we shorted the pound in the Quantum Fund. I didn't know whether the pound was going to devalue.

What I did know was that if they didn't devalue in the next 6 months, my fund was going to lose 50 basis points.

If they did devalue, I was going to make 2000 basis points. So it was a 40-1 one-way risk-reward bet.

BREXIT

I'm very good friends with Johann Rupert.

He told me he calls her "Mrs T" and that's Margaret Thatcher. He said, *When I met with Mrs T, she said never underestimate the common sense of the British people.*

I just felt that they were not going to go for socialism and frankly, when I look at what's going on in Europe and when I look at what's going on in Britain, I was always a Brexiteer.

They did perfectly fine for 500 years without that union of countries down there who seemed all to hate each other and they can't make a decision on anything.

So I think this is going to be actually very good for the British economy. I separate myself from most on that.

I think Boris Johnson is sort of a smarter version of Trump without some of the antics to go along with it.

BULL MARKET GENIUSES

I think there's a lot of bull market geniuses around and it's not that they love the game, they love winning but they were surfing with a hurricane behind their back that was giving them their nice waves.

They may become very discouraged.

YOUNG ENERGY

I love being around kids.

I couldn't figure out why all these 70 year olds wanted to hang out with me when I was 27.

Now I understand, and I'm trying to steal their energy from them like they stole from me at the time.

When I got promoted to director of equity research, Speros asked, "You know why I'm doing this, don't you?"

"No," I replied.

"For the same reason they send eighteen-year-olds into war."

"Why is that?" I asked.

"Because they're too dumb to know not to charge.

The small cap stocks have been in a bear market for ten years, and I think there's going to be a huge, liquidity-driven bull market sometime in the next decade.

Frankly, I have a lot of scars from the past ten years, while you don't.

I think we'll make a great team because you'll be too stupid and inexperienced to know not to try to buy everything. That other guy out there," he said, referring to my boss, the exiting director of equity research, "is just as stale as I am."

SUCCESSFUL INVESTING

The way to build long-term returns is through preservation of capital and home runs. We were expected to make 20% year in and year out no matter what the environment.

You can be far more aggressive when you're making good profits.

Many managers, once they're up 30 or 40 percent, will book their year.

The way to attain truly superior long-term returns is to grind it out until you're up 30 or 40 percent, and then if you have the convictions, go for a 100 percent year.

If you can put together a few near 100 percent years and avoid down years, then you can achieve really outstanding long-term returns.

I believe that good investors are successful not because of their IQ, but because they have an investing discipline.

But, what is more disciplined than a machine?

A well-researched machine can make many average investors redundant, leaving behind only the really good human investors with exceptional intuition and skill.

I've always loved to play games, and face it: investing is one big game. You need to be decisive, open-minded, flexible and competitive.

Bulls make more money than bears so being an optimist about life and about things in general is a great attribute to have as an investor. You just can't be starry-eyed and not naive. A better characteristic also is being able to control your emotions.

You need to be intellectually curious, really, really open-minded and you need to have courage.

You need courage to bet big and bet concentrated, but also the courage to fight your own emotions.

I've never made a buy at a low that I didn't just feel terrible and scared to death making it. It's easy to sell at the bottom. You can go home that night and relives you of your nerves.

WHAT HAPPENS NEXT

In 45 years I've never seen a constellation while I was a practitioner or frankly studied one where there's no historical analog. So right now I probably have more humility in terms of my views going forward than I've had maybe ever. Between the pandemic, the war, and the crazy policy response in the US and worldwide, this is the hardest environment I've ever encountered to try and have any confidence in a forecast 6 to 12 months ahead.

There are brewing issues when you get the price of oil doing what it's doing historically, you get interest rates what they're doing historically, and it becomes a global phenomenon with tightening liquidity and you've got war.

When I look back at the bull market we've been in financial assets which really started in 1982 and particularly in the last 10 years it went into hyperdrive. All the factors that created that not only have stopped, they have reversed.

The odds of a global recession and a change in the macro economy are about as high and as severe as I've seen them in decades.

We had a government back then where the new president who said *Government is not the solution, they're the problem.*

We had a guy who wanted to deregulate as oppose to regulate.

We had a Chairman of the Federal Reserve named Paul Volcker, little different then Jerome Powell.

Maybe most importantly, we were right on the cusp of globalization that led to one world, a lot of productivity, disinflation.

The response after the global financial crisis to that disinflation was 0 rates, a lot of money printing, and quantitative easing that created an asset bubble in everything.

Now they're like reform smokers. They've gone from

driving a Porsche 200 miles an hour to not only taking the foot off the gas but just slamming the brakes on.

There's a high probability that the market at best is going to be flat for 10 years like the '66 — '82 time period. The nice thing is there were companies that did very well in that environment back then. That's when Apple Computers were founded, Home Depot was founded, coal, energy and chemical companies made a lot of money in the '70s.

In 2009, I made a statement inside the firm that was, *we won't have another financial crisis for another 30 or 40 years because once you have one of these everyone learns from it and we get discipline and it takes them that long to screw up again.* The last one we had was obviously '29.

I'm not so sure I buy into all this stuff about bank balance sheets and this and that. What the central banks globally have done the last 10 or 11 years.

Think of the '30s — a post asset bubble. Just absolute destruction in buying power going forward. And then do we have the fed pump it all up again and we get some kind of horrible stagflation thing or do we actually get deflation.

Somebody always asks is this going to end in inflation or deflation. I don't know — 70% inflation and 30% deflation.

We've never had an inflation because we're too close to the zero bound. Every deflation has followed an asset bubble. And since the Fed has created the biggest asset bubble, even though a lot of air has been let out of the balloon, it's so big I just have to be open-minded about the consequences.

We've had two really bad ones in the last hundred years — the US in the 20's and Japan in '89 (they're still suffering). So it could just be no growth and sideways for 15 or 20 years like '66 to '82 in terms of the markets or it could be something more pernicious like we had in Japan.

Frankly, I don't know. I'm just trying to be open-minded.

If you look at the liquidity situation that has driven this, we're going to go from all of this [quantitative easing] to [quantitative tightening], we've been running down the [strategic petroleum reserve], it's now below '84 levels, even though obviously oil consumption is much higher now.

We've had a bunch of myopic policies that have actually delayed the liquidity shrinkage. QT has been almost entirely offset by Janet Yellen running down the Treasury savings account. She could have sold 10 years for under 1% during this time. Instead she runs down the Treasury savings account. All of that has masked liquidity shrinkage. She can continue this for a while. We can do the SPR for a while. Stimulative stuff.

But by the first quarter of 2023, it goes the other way.

Our central case is a hard landing by the end of 2023.

DEBT CRISIS AND ENTITLEMENT FUNDING

We're in deep trouble.

The only thing Donald Trump and Hillary Clinton agreed on in 2016 was don't cut social security, don't cut entitlements.

So nothing was done.

Joe Biden has excoriated Rick Scott because he dared mention maybe we shouldn't be increasing [at the current pace].

But if you look at the reversal I just talked about and you use the CBO estimate, which is rates at 3.8 percent, which I think is pretty optimistic given all the things we've talked about, by 2027 the interest expense alone on the debt eats all health care spending.

By 2047, it eats all discretionary spending. We're now getting into fiscal dominance. By 2049 it eats all Social Security.

We're getting to the point now where the interest expense on the debt is so high that it's going to eat up our ability to basically service the next generation, and I'm not even sure about the current one.

We better not all live forever because our kids won't have any money because they'll be paying our Social Security.

UNCERTAINTY

[You] don't even need to talk about black swans to be worried here.

To me, the risk-reward of owning assets doesn't make a lot of sense.

I'm not advocating going short.

The greatest short seller ever, Jesse Livermore, made $100 million in '29, and then he went bankrupt in '36 and killed himself.

I don't think you need to short.

Just sidestep it. To me the risk-reward is difficult right now.

CATALYST FOR CHANGE

My first boss in Pittsburgh in 1976 said, "Stanley, the way you time a political cycle is you buy the market two years before the general election and then you sell it on the general election, because they always rig things to be good in the election year."

He said this in '76.

We had major bottoms in '78, '82, '86, '90, '94, '98, '02, not so much in '06 because Bush tried to push it through all the way, and we see what happens.

The incredible thing about the myopic policies they're running, and I assume it's for the midterms, is it's kind of dumb politically because it sets up a bad '24.

Maybe the silver lining is we get a crisis that doesn't destroy us but it's bad enough maybe to bring us together and someone comes out of nowhere.

We definitely need a change. Half the country hates the other half.

We've got myopic economic policies, boom-bust policies.

You don't really get change unless bad stuff happens to catalyze the change.

That's what brought in Paul Volcker, G. William Miller, and Arthur Burns preceded him.

So as gloomy as I am, I'm open to something really great happening out of nowhere that we don't see catalyzed by something bad before it happens.

THE SUPER INVESTOR SERIES

Tiger Management, the hedge fund founded by billionaire investor Julian Robertson, had a practice of giving their new analysts a short and sweet primer on investing lessons they had learned. This little booklet was filled with quotes from super investors. Here's one such quote:

When you're making money, you're not as smart as you feel.

When you're losing money, you're also not as stupid.

The goal of the Super Investor Series is to give you the same primer in the form of gold nuggets from legendary investors.

Books in the Super Investor Series:

- *The Almanack of Jim Chanos*
- *The Almanack of Michael Burry*
- *The Almanack of Jim Simons*
- *The Almanack of Ed Thorp*
- *The Almanack of Stanley Druckenmiller*

• *Charlie Munger: The Pursuit of Worldly Wisdom*

Bonus content available on SuperInvestorSeries.com

Made in the USA
Las Vegas, NV
21 December 2022